At the
Health Centre

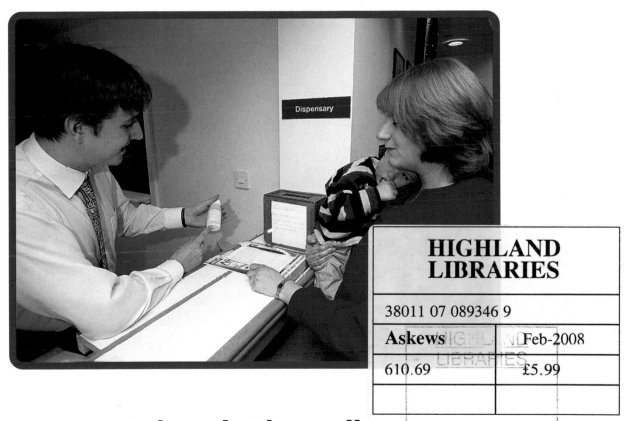

Deborah Chancellor

Photographs: Chris Fairclough

W
FRANKLIN WATTS
LONDON•SYDNEY

This symbol is often seen on ambulances and medical signs. The snake and staff (the stick in the middle) are the symbols of Asclepius, the Ancient Greek god of healing.

This edition 2007

First published in 2003 by
Franklin Watts
338 Euston Road
London NW1 3BH

Franklin Watts Australia
Level 17/207 Kent Street
Sydney NSW 2000

© Franklin Watts 2003
Dewey Decimal Classification Number 362.1'4

ISBN 978 0 7496 7270 6
Dewey Decimal Classification Number 363.2

Series Editor: Jackie Hamley
Cover Design: Peter Scoulding
Design: Ian Thompson

Photos
All commissioned photographs by Chris Fairclough.
The publishers would like to thank the following
for permission to use photographs:
John Birdsall Photo Library p. 27 top and bottom

Every attempt has been made to clear copyright. Should there be any
inadvertent omission, please apply to the publisher for rectification.

The author and publisher would especially like to thank everyone at
Linton Health Centre for giving their help and time so generously.

Printed in Malaysia

Franklin Watts is a division of Hachette Children's Books.

Contents

Meet the team

We go to a health centre when we are sick and need to see a doctor or nurse.

Many different people work together in health centres. These people work at the Linton Health Centre in Cambridgeshire in England.

These people are medical staff. They are experts at looking after people's health.

Doctors: **1** Luis Videl **2** Jonathan Silverman
3 Natasha Ray **4** James Hewlett **5** Pennie Tewson
6 Roger Bertram **7** Miguel Arbide **8** Roger Petter
9 Jo Farnell
Physiotherapist: **10** Jane
Nursery nurse: **11** Pauline
Health visitors: **12** Marilyn   **13** Sue
Practice nurses: **14** Sue **15** Claire **16** Hazel
Community mental health nurse: **17** Hilary
Phlebotomist: **18** Jan   Midwife: **19** Marilyn
District nurse: **20** Siobhan   Pharmacist: **21** Jody

Each person has a part in looking after the patients and making sure the health centre runs smoothly.

The doctors, nurses and other medical staff take care of the health of the patients.
The office staff include receptionists, a secretarial assistant, a computer administrator and an **audit clerk**. The housekeeper keeps the building clean and tidy. The practice manager looks after the day-to-day running of the health centre.

This group of people help the medical staff do their jobs.

Receptionists: **1** Irene
2 Sally **3** Carol **4** Jan
5 Eileen (senior receptionist)
Secretarial assistant: **6** Jo
Computer administrator: **7** Gilly
Dispensers: **8** Judith **9** Judy
10 Norma
Audit clerk: **11** Isobel
Housekeeper: **12** Mary
Practice manager: **13** Sheila

The health centre

Linton Health Centre is a very busy place. It looks after 11,000 patients. The staff work hard to help them all.

The health centre opens at 8 o'clock in the morning. The receptionists and the office staff are always in by this time. Sheila, the practice manager, is one of the first to arrive.

Sheila's job is to make sure the health centre runs smoothly, every day of the year.

The receptionists start their day by answering the phones. Many patients phone the health centre early in the morning to make an appointment.

The receptionists book the first patients in to see the doctors at 8.30 in the morning.

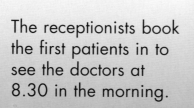

The health centre's office is next to the reception desk. The people who work there keep the health centre well organised.

Jo is the secretarial assistant in the office. She opens all the health centre's post every morning.

Jo sorts out the post and makes sure each letter is given to the right member of staff.

> **Sometimes I open hundreds of letters in one morning. It takes me a few hours to sort them all out.**
>
> **Jo, secretarial assistant**

New patients

To see a doctor or nurse at the health centre, you have to be registered there.

Nick has just moved to Linton and needs to find a new doctor. He fills in a **registration form** at the health centre reception desk, giving information about his health.

The information on Nick's form will be very useful to his new doctor.

Gilly checks that all new patients are registered properly and that their details are correct.

Nick's **medical records** will be sent to Linton Health Centre by his old doctor. Gilly, the computer administrator, enters Nick's details onto the computer.

All the patients' medical records are kept in a large filing area. The records are kept in alphabetical order, starting with surnames beginning with "a", and ending with those beginning with "z".

Carol, one of the receptionists, puts Nick's medical records in the right place, so they are easy to find next time.

Making an appointment

■ People usually make an appointment to see the doctors or nurses at the health centre.

Now that he has registered, Nick wants to make an appointment to see his doctor. Carol, one of the receptionists, checks the appointments on her computer.

Carol tries to find a time when Nick's doctor is free.

> *We answer about 40 phone calls between 8.30 and 10 o'clock in the morning. Most of these calls are from people who want to make an appointment with a doctor or nurse.*
>
> **Carol, receptionist**

When patients arrive for an appointment, they give their name to a receptionist. Then they wait in the waiting room until the doctor or nurse is ready to see them.

Patients do not usually have to wait too long. If delays happen, they are for good reasons. For example, an emergency patient may arrive and need to be fitted in between booked appointments.

Dr Arbide has just finished seeing a patient. He calls out his next patient's name.

Patients can read magazines while they wait.

Children play in a special play area next to the waiting room.

⬛ **Every morning before surgery, the doctors read their appointment lists. These tell the doctors who is coming to see them.**

The doctors need the medical records of each patient they see. The receptionists sort out the medical records, ready for the doctors to use.

Dr Petter will not have to waste time during his surgery looking for patients' medical records.

Dr Petter's first patient is Joe who has earache. Dr Petter looks in Joe's ear and sees he has an ear **infection**.

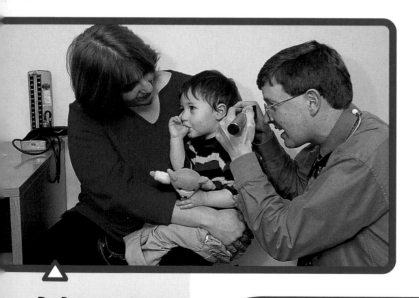

Dr Petter inspects Joe's ear with an instrument called an auriscope.

> *I normally see about 30 patients a day, in booked appointments. I also see a few emergency patients, who need to see a doctor straight away.*
> **Dr Petter**

Dr Petter writes down the name of some medicine that will help Joe's ear. A doctor's written request for medicine is called a **prescription**.

Dr Petter's prescription is for **antibiotics**. Antibiotics are drugs that can get rid of some infections.

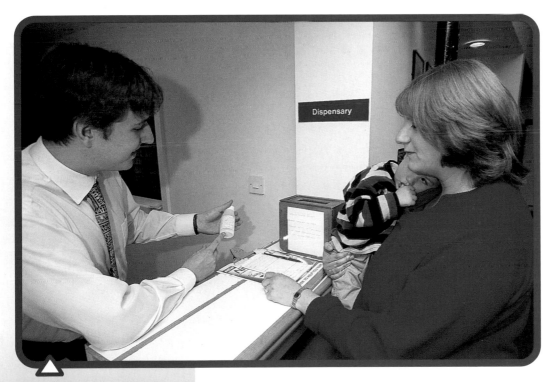

The **pharmacist** explains to Joe's mum when the antibiotics should be taken.

Joe's mum takes the prescription to the health centre **dispensary**. This is where patients can pick up their medicines.

Doctor on call

Some patients are too sick to travel to the health centre. They need to see a doctor at home.

In the office, Jo, the secretarial assistant, answers phone calls from patients who want a doctor to visit them at home.

Jo writes down the patients' details to give to the doctors.

After morning surgery, the doctors check the requests for home visits. They phone some of the patients to give advice. Then they arrange visits for the patients who need to see them.

Doctors also have to phone hospitals to arrange for some patients to see other specialist doctors.

The doctors only have time to visit the most urgent cases at home.

Doctors fit in two or three home visits a day between morning and afternoon surgery.

FACT

What to do if you need a doctor when the surgery is closed:

▶ *Phone the health centre.*

▶ *Listen to the recorded message.*

▶ *Write down the telephone number of the emergency reception.*

▶ *Phone this number and give your telephone number.*

▶ *The doctor on call will phone you to arrange a home visit.*

Dr Petter is going to visit one of his patients at home. He takes a big case with the equipment he may need to help the patient.

When Dr Petter is "on call" he may even have to make home visits in the middle of the night!

The practice nurses

The nurses at the health centre are called practice nurses. They help some patients and also give health advice.

The **practice nurses** see patients by appointment, just like the doctors. There are two nurses' surgery rooms at the health centre, which are busy all day long.

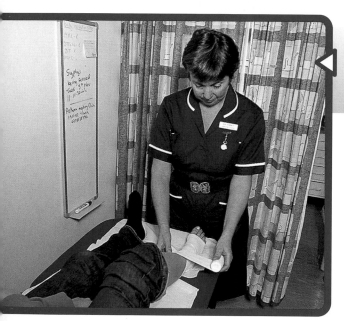

Practice nurses spend lots of time putting **dressings** on patients' cuts and burns.

A **phlebotomist** works with the practice nurses. Phlebotomists take blood from patients so it can be tested. The results of a blood test can help doctors find out what is wrong with a patient.

Jan is a phlebotomist. She looks after her blood testing equipment very carefully. Most of it can only be used once, then it has to be thrown away.

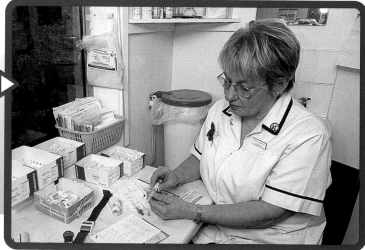

The practice nurses also give **immunisations**. If you are immunised against an illness such as flu, you are protected from catching that illness. Young children are immunised against some illnesses before they start school.

The **vaccines** used to give immunisations are kept in a fridge near the nurses' surgery.

Young children are given a sticker after their immunisations.

Anna, Siobhan and Heather are district nurses. They meet in their office to arrange some home visits.

Some patients need medical care quite often, but are unable to go to the health centre. This might be because they are too old or too sick. **District nurses** look after these patients, and visit them in their own homes.

The asthma clinic

The practice nurses run several clinics at the health centre. The clinics are for people with medical conditions such as asthma.

Isobel has a list on her computer of all the patients with asthma.

It is important that all patients with **asthma** are invited to come to a clinic. Isobel, the audit clerk in the office, makes sure that this happens.

At the asthma clinic, the nurses help patients understand their breathing problems, and tell them what to do to keep well.

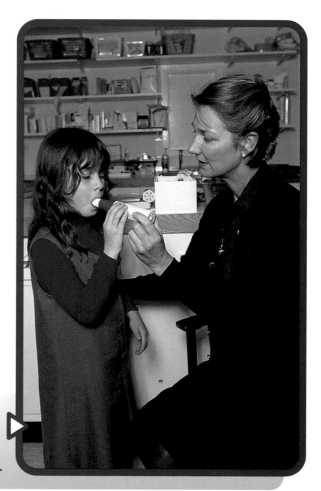

Charlotte is breathing into a peak flow meter. This equipment shows how much of her lungs she uses when she breathes.

Claire shows Charlotte how to use her inhaler properly, by breathing in deeply.

Nurse Claire shows patients how to use inhalers to control their asthma. Some inhalers help prevent asthma, and some help you to breathe if you have an asthma attack.

By seeing her asthma patients regularly, Claire can make sure that they are using the right inhaler for their asthma.

FACT

▷ Asthma affects one in seven children.

▷ The number of children with asthma goes up every year.

▷ Asthma is often brought on by an allergy to something.

▷ Some experts think pollution can cause asthma in children.

The baby clinic

■ Health visitors are also called children's community nurses. They look after children and young families.

Carolyn asks the health visitor for some advice about feeding her baby.

The **health visitors** at Linton Health Centre hold a baby clinic twice a week. Carolyn is worried that her baby, Tilly, is not gaining enough weight. She has brought Tilly to the baby clinic to be weighed.

Baby Tilly is just two weeks old. Sue, the health visitor, puts her on some scales to check that she is growing and gaining weight properly.

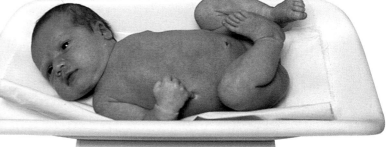

Babies are weighed without their nappies on, because this gives a more accurate result. Tilly's weight is shown on the dark screen.

At the baby clinic, the health visitors give check-ups to all babies when they are six weeks and eight months old. If there seems to be a problem, the babies are also seen by a doctor at the health centre.

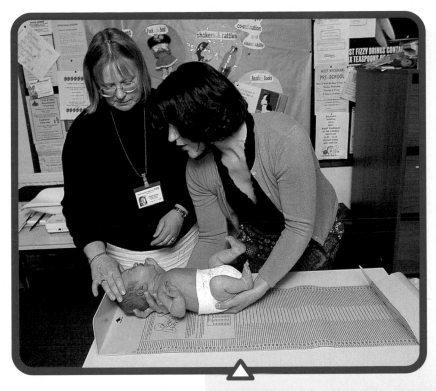

Tilly is measured on a special mat. Babies are "long", not "tall", because they can't stand up to be measured.

Marilyn, the **midwife**, works with the health visitors at the health centre. She sees pregnant mothers at the health centre, and helps them give birth at the local hospital. For the first couple of weeks after the birth, she visits the families at home.

Marilyn is leaving the health centre to visit a newborn baby at home. She has some weighing scales in her big case.

The dispensary

Linton Health Centre has its own dispensary. A dispensary gives out medicines that have been prescribed by a doctor.

Many of the patients at Linton Health Centre do not live near a pharmacy. They use the health centre's dispensary to get the medicines they need.

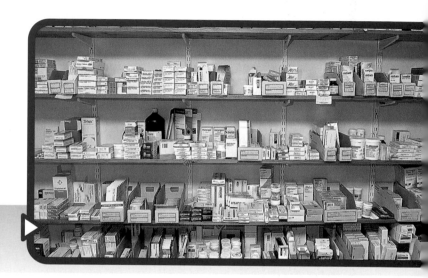

Lots of different drugs are stored in the dispensary.

The dispensers measure out the correct amount of medicine for each patient.

The people who work in the dispensary are called **dispensers**. They read the prescriptions and sort out the right medicines for the patients. The dispensers work quickly, so patients do not have to wait too long to pick up their medicines.

Jody is the pharmacist in charge of the dispensary. He answers any questions that patients may have about their medicines, and how they work.

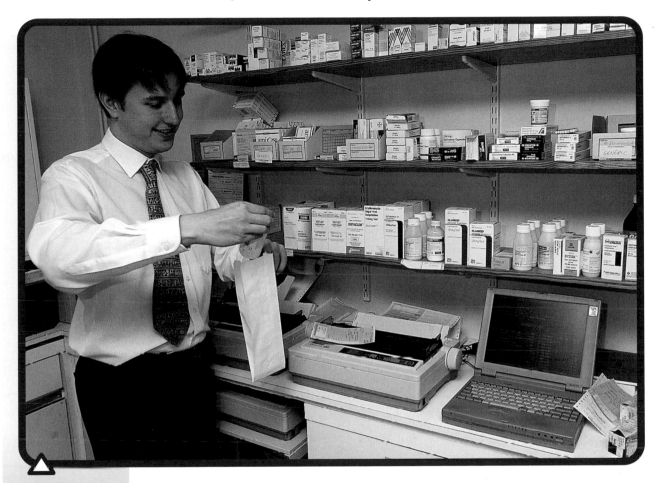

Sometimes Jody gives advice to the doctors about new medicines.

"*People often ask me how their medicine will affect them. Some medicines can make people feel a bit different, for example more tired than usual.*

Jody, pharmacist"

Health education

■ **We need to learn how to look after our bodies. There are some things we can do to help us keep well.**

The health visitors at the health centre are keen to teach people about healthy living. They visit lots of schools and youth clubs to talk to children.

The health visitors have an office in the health centre.

Sue and Marilyn are health visitors, and Pauline is a nursery nurse. They meet together to plan their visits to the local schools. When they go into a school, they talk about healthy eating and exercise.

The health visitors explain how important it is to eat five portions of fruit and vegetables every day. They also try to persuade children to cut down on fat, salt and sugar in their **diet**.

Eating a lot of fast food is bad for your health.

The health visitors encourage children to get as much exercise as possible. This might mean walking to school or taking up a new sport.

Having exercise is not only good for you, it can be fun, too.

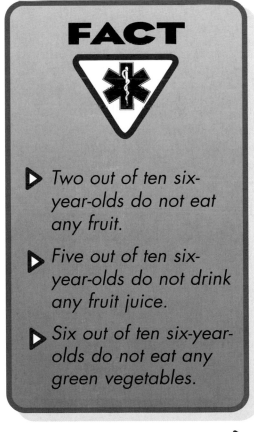

FACT

▷ *Two out of ten six-year-olds do not eat any fruit.*

▷ *Five out of ten six-year-olds do not drink any fruit juice.*

▷ *Six out of ten six-year-olds do not eat any green vegetables.*

Staying healthy

■ If you want to stay healthy, you must eat and drink sensibly. This means eating different kinds of food and drinking lots of water.

■ Try to eat something from each of the following food groups, every day:

1. Protein Food with protein builds up your body. Protein can be found in meat, fish, nuts, eggs, milk and cheese.

2. Carbohydrates Carbohydrates give you energy. They can be found in rice, pasta and potatoes.

3. Fats Fats help you store up energy. They are found in nuts, meat and dairy foods.

4. Vitamins Vitamins and minerals keep your body working properly. They are found in fruit, vegetables, liver and milk.

5. Fibre Food with fibre helps your body get rid of waste. Fibre can be found in brown bread and bananas.

■ There are many reasons why you should exercise. Here are the main ones:

1. Being active helps your bones and muscles grow.

2. Your heart and lungs work better when you take exercise.

3. Keeping fit gives you lots of energy and makes you feel good.

Glossary

antibiotics Drugs used to kill germs and cure infections.

asthma People with asthma have breathing problems. The tubes which carry air to and from their lungs become narrow, making it hard to breathe.

audit clerk An office worker at the health centre who keeps track of patients with health conditions, such as asthma.

diet The food that you normally eat.

dispensary The place where patients can pick up medicine that has been prescribed by a doctor.

dispenser Someone who works in a dispensary, giving out prescribed medicines.

district nurse A nurse who visits patients who can't get to the health centre.

dressing A covering for a wound, for example a bandage.

health visitor A nurse who looks after young children and their families.

immunisation An immunisation against an illness stops you from catching that illness. Immunisations are usually given by an injection.

infection An illness caused by germs.

medical records A patient's medical records give details of all the illnesses and medical problems the patient has had.

midwife A nurse who helps mothers give birth to and care for their babies.

pharmacist The pharmacist is in charge of the dispensary.

phlebotomist Someone who is trained to take blood samples.

practice nurse A nurse who works in general practice, not in a hospital.

prescription A doctor's written request for medicine.

registration form To become a new patient at the health centre, you must answer the questions on this form.

vaccine A substance used to give people immunisations.

Further information

To find out more about how to look after your health, you can visit:

www.welltown.gov.uk

www.lifebytes.gov.uk

To find out more about health education in Australia, visit:

www.healthstar.com.au

The British Nutrition Foundation gives people information about healthy eating.

You can write to the Foundation at this address:

British Nutrition Foundation
High Holborn House
52–54 High Holborn
London
WC1V 6RQ

visit: www.nutrition.org.uk
or telephone: (020) 7404 6504

Note to parents and teachers: Every effort has been made by the Publishers to ensure that these websites are suitable for children; that they are of the highest educational value, and that they contain no inappropriate or offensive material. However, because of the nature of the Internet, it is impossible to guarantee that the contents of these sites will not be altered. We strongly advise that Internet access is supervised by a responsible adult.

Index